GW01086967

AUNT MARGARET'S PUDDING

AUNT MARGARET'S PUDDING

Poems inspired by a handwritten notebook of recipes from Dorothy Eliza Barnes (Dot), my grandmother, a shepherd's wife, who had worked as an Edwardian cook.

Alison Brackenbury

HAPPENSTANCE

ISBN 978-1-910131-43-5

ACKNOWLEDGMENTS:

Thanks are due to the editors of the the following publications, in which some of these poems first appeared: *Clear Poetry, The New Statesman, The North, The Spectator.*

By the same author:

Alison Brackenbury is the author of nine previous book-length collections published by Carcanet Press. The most recent of these is *Skies*, Carcanet 2016. A pamphlet, *Shadow*, was published by Happen*Stance* Press in 2009.

NOTE FOR VISUALLY IMPAIRED READERS:

The book jacket is pale blue. Lettering on the front cover is centred and dark blue. The author's name appears first in lower-case italics, followed by the title ('AUNT MARGARET'S PUDDING') in large caps. Below this is a hand-drawn graphic on a grass-green background, showing a steamed pudding on a plate with red jam trickling down the sides and curls of steam rising. The pudding is surrounded by ingredients: raspberry jam, yellow butter, creamy eggs (one cracked open), white sugar, a blue packet of flour, and some utensils: a spoon, a sieve, a balloon whisk. A few raspberries are scattered here and there. On the back jacket, beside the blurb, is an oval monochrome photo of Dot, the central subject of the book (same photo as on title page). It shows Dot at about 17, in a smart jacket with flowery lapels and white high-necked blouse fastened with a brooch. Her hair is swept back in a bun. She has a clear, steady gaze and sweet expression.

Printed and bound by Imprint Digital, Exeter
https://digital.imprint.co.uk

First published in 2018 by Happen*Stance* Press,
21 Hatton Green, Glenrothes, Fife KY7 4SD
nell@happenstancepress.com
www.happenstancepress.com

CONTENTS

Aunt Margarets Pudding.

½ lb flour. 3 oz lard or butter ¼ lb sugar
1 teaspoon B.P. mix with one egg and
a little milk. Put a layer of jam at
bottom of basin. Steam 1½ hrs.

START

Page one: *Aunt Margaret's Pudding.*
Take half a pound of flour,
three ounces lard (or butter), egg,
milk, sugar, baking powder.
Spread jam in basin, summer gleam.
Poke fire! For ninety minutes, steam.

Dot took for granted custard seas,
in which all puddings swam—
yellow as straw, farmworkers' food.
In frost, the men tramped home.
Moon glittered. No one knew how lard
would line and leave their arteries hard.

When I came home and you worked late,
our workshop gloomed with cold,
I bought flour from the corner shop
sacked cupboards for old bowls.
Softly the mixture dropped. I too
spooned Margaret's hot jam sponge for you.

Aunt Margaret's Pudding

DOT'S ORIGINAL RECIPE

½ lb flour. 3 oz lard or butter ¼ lb sugar
1 teaspoon B.P. mix with one egg and
a little milk. Put a layer of jam at
bottom of basin Steam 1½ hrs.

My version:

INGREDIENTS

4 oz / 120 g self-raising flour
1½ oz / 45 g butter or lard, slightly softened
2 oz / 60 g golden caster sugar
1 medium egg
A little milk if needed
Some good quality, home-made jam

EQUIPMENT

1 pt / 568 ml pudding basin
Greaseproof paper and also foil
String
Large saucepan big enough to contain the pudding basin easily.

NOTE:
If you haven't made a steamed pudding before, check online for a video demo of how to butter the greaseproof paper, pleat it, cover with similarly pleated foil, tie with string, etc. It is not hard, but helps to watch someone else do it the first time.

METHOD

1. Butter the pudding basin.
2. Put generous layer of jam at bottom of basin.
3. Weigh softened fat, cut into small pieces and put into a mixing bowl.
4. Weigh sugar and add to butter.
5. Cream butter and sugar until pale and fluffy.
6. Sift and weigh flour.
7. Beat egg. Mix ½ egg and all the flour lightly into the butter & sugar mix.
8. Add rest of egg gradually until mixture is soft enough to spoon into the bowl (add a little milk if needed). Combine ingredients thoroughly but do not overmix.
9. Spoon pudding mixture into basin on top of jam. Smooth top of mixture.
10. Place greaseproof and foil over the top and tie string round firmly.
11. Place in a large saucepan with enough simmering water to come half way up the basin. Put lid on tightly. Simmer on low heat for 1½ hours (but keep a wary eye that water doesn't evaporate). Or, if you have a steamer, cook on top layer following steamer instructions for the same length of time.
12. When pudding is done (you can test with a skewer inserted through the foil), uncover and turn onto a plate. The jam will dribble beautifully over the top and—be careful—will be extraordinarily hot.
13. Serve with custard (or cream).

ALL CHANGE

In schoolgirl hand and blackest black
you scratched down with your steel nib
Puzzle Pudding, Feather Cake
in neat fast script, no time to think.
Now sky-blue strays into the mix,
light as fire through kindling sticks.
Pencil races. *Elderberry.*
Then biro shakes. No more splashed ink.

B.P. was baking powder. Why?
Did slick self-raising come too late?
Nor did you have penicillin,
pethidine, or the Welfare State.
Cake with dried egg. You barely paused,
queued, improvised, cooked through two wars.
Slow oven. By my birth, you could
swap coal for cooker, need not wait.

Still you kept adding recipes,
lighter, not heavy, blue, not black.
From *Woman's Own* came 'Chocolate Cake'.
The '60s cooled upon your rack.
With sister, daughter dead, you made
fine curds, great pies, long table laid.
Why did you never show me this?
Beat four eggs well. Do not look back.

HIGH-CLASS FOOD

Both my grandmothers were of age
to stuff fat sausages with sage,
Lincolnshire's herb which calms the blood.

They could make dumplings sweet with suet,
slash egg-white with a knife till thick,
plate shoulder-poised (Victorian trick)

but never dreamed of kneading bread.
They ran to bakers' vans instead.

Yet when strange men tramped round the farms
to beg for work in '30s storms
Dot—between her jobs—would pour

sweetened tea for them before
sending them out in rain well-fed
on home-cured bacon and white bread.

Raspberry Buns

DOT'S ORIGINAL RECIPE

6 oz G. rice 6 oz flour, 4 oz butter 4 oz sugar, 1 teaspoon B.P.
Mix into a stiff paste with one egg and a little milk.
Divide into balls hollow each and insert
a little raspberry jam and close up again.
Bake in a sharp oven.

My version:

(Makes about 10 buns)

INGREDIENTS

3 oz / 90 g ground rice
3 oz / 90 g self-raising flour
2 oz / 60 g butter
2 oz / 60 g caster sugar
1 medium egg
A little milk if needed
Raspberry jam

EQUIPMENT

Baking tray or preferably mince pie tin.
Greaseproof paper or baking parchment.

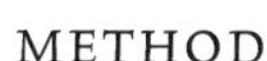

METHOD

1. Grease baking tray or mince pie tin well.
2. Pre-heat oven to 190°C/ 375°F/ Gas Mark 5 (Dot's 'sharp oven'!)
3. Sieve flour and ground rice into a bowl and rub in butter cut into small pieces.
4. Stir in sugar. Add beaten egg gradually to make a fairly stiff consistency that you can mould with fingers. (The more egg/ liquid you add, the more your buns will spread and flatten.)
5. Roll paste lightly into a sausage. Divide into 9/10 pieces.
6. Mould pieces into balls with your fingers. Hollow out the centre of each with your finger, making a little cave.
7. Place balls into mince pie tin. If using a flat baking tray, allow generous space between them.
8. Insert a generous teaspoon of raspberry jam into the 'cave' in the heart of each bun.
9. Pinch hole closed again (a little of the dough is useful to lay over and seal the top).
10. Bake for about 15 minutes till golden brown.
11. Cool on a wire rack.
12. A sprinkling of icing sugar sieved over the top makes them look festive (though Dot would not have countenanced this).

CLEAN

Even their daughters could not know
quite how they did it. They had learnt
to brush, beat, polish for the rich
who picked at toast, yawned at each stitch.
Dot's own rooms smelled of coal tar soap,
cool as sea, brown as petals, burnt.

She stored black notebooks in her drawer
with 'recipes' her mother tried.
For feverish children, scoured by food,
rhubarb and *laudmum* were thought good:
a purge. (They needed water more,
salts, to revive. They may have died.)

Their small ghosts crowded in her mind.
The enemy would not retire.
Floors, kitchen table, sinks were scrubbed
till acid-pale, unpolished, tough.
(I dab bleach.) Aching, she would find
mud from men's boots, ash from the fire.

My father saw her climb a chair.
Arms, dark as chimney, sluiced each beam.
She never glimpsed my calm dust. Still,
come Christmas, snows of polish fill
her deep black spoons for spices, flour.
Find rags. Rub tarnish. Hold her gleam.

INGREDIENTS

Carrots kept Christmas pudding plain.
No gold leaf flattered Nottingham.
Choclate—you wrote, brisk, young.
What sweetness touched your tongue?

Your first friends were cornflour, ground rice.
Your middle age still sang with spice,
spooned, generous to a fault.
Cinnamon. Ginger. *Salt?*

Steam smudged your letters. *Leather Cups?*
I squint. The words are: *Quaker Oats.*
Your trust in brand names shone.
King, Country, only one.

You knew dessert. You wrote
the old name: *cocoanut.*
Through bright *Treacle* I see
the dark Imperial tree.

A married student, money short,
I spooned rough ground rice at the start—
strong, workaday, low-cost—
like all the tastes we lost.

Quaker Oat Scones

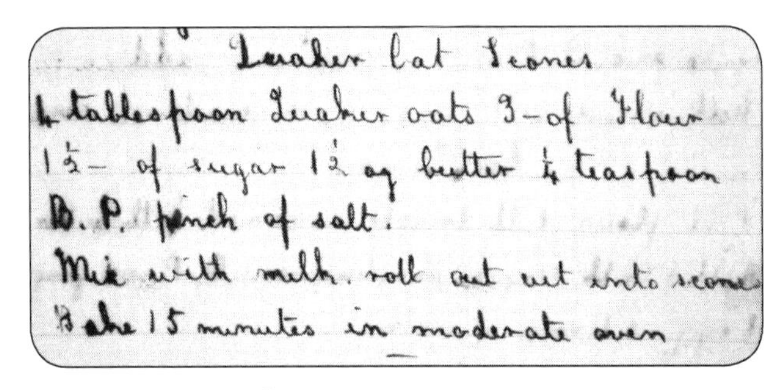
Quaker Oat Scones
4 tablespoon Quaker oats 3 – of Flour
1½ – of sugar 1½ oz butter ¼ teaspoon
B.P. pinch of salt.
Mix with milk. roll out cut into scones
Bake 15 minutes in moderate oven

DOT'S ORIGINAL RECIPE

4 tablespoon Quaker oats 3 [oz] of Flour
1½ [oz] of sugar 1 ½[oz] of butter ¼ teaspoon
B.P. pinch of salt.
Mix with milk, roll out out into scones.
Bake 15 minutes in moderate oven

Thanks to the oats, whose brand name Dot includes with such reverence, these scones have a lighter and crisper consistency than many others.

My version:
(makes about 5 medium scones)

INGREDIENTS

4 heaped tablespoons of porridge oats
3 oz / 100 g self-raising flour
1½ oz / 50 g caster sugar
1½ oz / 50 g butter
Pinch of salt and a little milk to mix.

EQUIPMENT

Rolling pin
Baking tray
Pastry cutters

METHOD

1. Pre-heat oven to 180°C/ 350°F/ Gas Mark 4.
2. Grease baking tray.
3. Weigh and sieve flour, add salt, mix.
4. Rub the chopped butter lightly into the flour with finger tips.
5. Stir sugar and oats into the mixture..
6. Add milk cautiously, mixing with a knife until mixture binds in a firm ball.
7. Turn scone dough out onto a lightly floured surface.
8. Gently flatten with lightly floured rolling pin.
9. Roll it out carefully until roughly as thick as the top joint of your thumb.
10. Cut into scones with scone cutter or knife.
11. Glaze top of each scone with a little milk or beaten egg.
12. Place scones, evenly spaced, on baking tray and put in oven.
13. Check after 12 minutes. They will be light gold all over when done.
14. Eat (preferably slightly warm) with butter.

DOT

But you were tiny. Not one toe
could stretch from sofa to the floor.
Unwise to marry a tall man? For
the fourth child left you bed-bound, so
kind neighbours cooked. Your eyes were weak,
yet blue as harebells. You would go
sleepless, to cram old trunks with cake
the men took to the Royal Show.

I have one picture, leather-bound:
you as a young, still-anxious cook,
flowered velvet in your collar's tuck.
Like food, you could make cash go round.
Only your hair grew wild. Its fine
strong waves defied your careful buns.
French marigolds by your washing line
met cabbage, hoed by husband, sons.

You never cut your springing hair.
Time washed past you like rain, your skin
so soft a child's lips would sink in.
My face, rough from hill wind, stays bare
of blusher, gloss. No powder tins
littered your rooms. I stay up, too,
cook, type, as horizons dim.
My father said I looked like you.

SUMMER FRUIT

You whisked meringues, light pancakes lest
Madam woke bored. You did not write
two recipes I loved the best

that dark blancmange, named *Chocolate Mould*,
which, young paid cook, you once coaxed whole
from fluted copper's fragrant gold,

then spooned, for us, from your gilt dish.
African nights caressed slow tongues.
We tasted empires, bitter, rich.

How could you find fruit in that flat
unflowered land? Air bloomed. You caught
the Barton bus, in your best hat.

Plum jam set August. Amber simmered
to slow taste, whole, spooned on warm sponge
as boots came off. Orion glimmered.

Summer, you said, for that Great War,
was like none after or before,
the loveliest you ever saw.

Bakewell Pudding

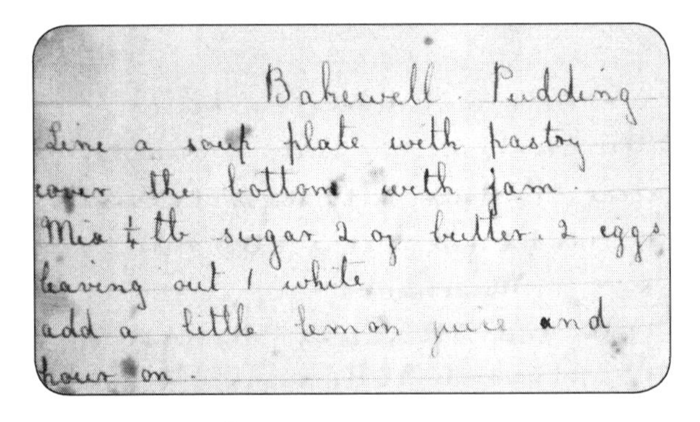
Bakewell Pudding
Line a soup plate with pastry
cover the bottom with jam.
Mix ¼ lb sugar 2 oz butter. 2 eggs
leaving out 1 white
add a little lemon juice and
pour on.

DOT'S ORIGINAL RECIPE

Line a soup plate with pastry
cover the bottom with jam.
Mix ¼ lb sugar 2 oz butter 2 eggs
leaving out 1 white
add a little lemon juice and
pour on.

This is a taste of history! Dot's notebook includes a fascinating version of a celebrated (officially secret) nineteenth-century recipe. You may have encountered Bakewell Tart. In modern versions—such as Mary Berry's—this is a jam-filled pastry case with a cake topping, heavily flavoured with almond, then topped with almonds and icing. It is very rich and sweet.

But, as a child, I was taken to an old coaching inn in Derbyshire where we ate 'Bakewell Pudding'. This was allegedly first made by accident in the 1860s, when a cook put some of the ingredients for a strawberry tart on top of her strawberries, instead of mixing them into a sweet pastry. The commercial makers of this pudding in Bakewell refuse to reveal their secrets. You can, however, find at least one very helpful re-creation on the Internet.

Dot's pudding definitely belongs to this famous family of traditional puddings. But hers has some striking differences. Unlike Mary Berry, and the Internet Bakewell enthusiasts, she creams her butter instead of melting it, and adds no almonds, real or synthetic. The result is characteristic of her cooking: both plain and delicate.

Dot's Bakewell Pudding has crisp pastry, topped by good jam, which is married to a moist top layer as yellow as buttercups, finely flavoured with lemon.

The top of her pudding, like the puddings made in Bakewell, is dark and crisp, as smoky as it is sweet. It is very good hot. I think it is even better cold: a classic English pudding. At the risk of being barred from Derbyshire, I have to say I prefer Dot's version to that now made in the inns of Bakewell!

For my version, see next page.

Bakewell Pudding: my version

INGREDIENTS

Pastry

You can use bought frozen short-crust pastry, or puff pastry, or make it as follows. The tip to mix self-raising and plain flour was given to me by Dot herself, with shy pride. It even improves my pastry. Hers was superb.

2 oz / 60 g self-raising flour
2 oz / 60 g plain flour
2 oz / 60 g butter
Pinch of salt
Cold water and a squeeze of lemon juice to mix

Filling

4 oz / 120 g golden caster sugar
2 oz / 60 g butter (softened)
1 whole egg + 1 egg yolk
Lemon juice to taste (about a dessertspoonful)
About 7 oz / 200 g of good jam.

EQUIPMENT

Wooden spoon
Rolling pin
7″ shallow cake tin or flan dish

Note:

Dot's pudding, like its traditional cousins, will rise spectacularly, then sink again. It is meant to—there's no flour in it. It is cooked when firm to the touch. Don't overcook or the top quickly burns. It is very different from most modern puddings, and curiously addictive. (The story of the confused cook is fine Victorian PR, but I wonder if this pudding is really much older.)

METHOD

Pastry:

1. Add salt to sieved flour, mix.
2. Chop chilled butter for pastry into the flour, and rub in with fingertips.
3. Add a little cold water gradually, and mix with knife, until mixture clings together.
4. Sieve a little flour on to the surface where you roll out the pastry.
5. Form the pastry into a ball and roll out to a thickness of about 4 mm.
6. Line your tin with the pastry, so it goes right up the sides to hold the topping.
7. Spread pastry with jam, right to the edge.
8. Pre-heat oven to 180°.

Filling

1. Cream butter and then beat in sugar till light and fluffy.
2. Beat whole egg and egg yolk together.
3. Add eggs gradually to butter and sugar mixture, beating well with each addition.
4. Beat in lemon juice.
5. Pour on top of the jam and pastry—quite quickly.
6. Cook for 30 minutes in pre-heated oven.

SAMPHIRE

Halfway down
Hangs one that gathers samphire—dreadful trade!
—Shakespeare, *King Lear*, Act 4, Scene 6

My grandmother could cook it, for
she grew up by that dangerous shore
where the sea skulked without a wall

where I have seen it, tough as grass,
where silent men with rods trooped past
its salty ranks, without a glance.

Lear's gatherer hangs perilously.
Why? So much is closed to me.
Did Shakespeare ever hear the sea?

Once, said my father, far inland,
from friend or stall, one clutch was found,
steamed, in my grandmother's great pan.

Later, a leaflet from a shop
claimed they could 'source it'. In its place
stood peppered cress—another gap.

Yet how it waved in late sea-light—
stalks I will never taste, but make
tenderly dark, my coast's sly snake,
salt on my tongue, before I wake.

LINCOLNSHIRE WATER

Here is strong land, whose grass
does not spill foaming milk,
where I still hear, in February,
taps hiss cold silk.

BUT

Their fourth child would leave women weak,
Dot's last, who proved, too briefly, bright.
No brightness in long labour, weeks
in bed, torn raw. Good neighbours cooked.
Last children chanced from one lost night,
the farmer's Christmas whisky. Look

at her, the framed cook, with sleeked hair,
then with three children, in a field.
Lack of sleep blacks her eyes. The air
tugs at her hasty bun. And he
thin as tobacco shreds; at heel
the collie, well-fed as the baby.

She knitted, hemmed. She lit, at dawn,
slow coppers, pounded dolly pegs
into the snarling sheets, tramped down
three miles to school, the youngest kept
in jolting pram to save his legs.
She scoured the sink. Sometimes, she slept.

Women keep silence after wars.
Dot would not speak of what went wrong.
My father never knew the cause
of surgery, but knew she should,
with two men out at work, too long,
not wield her axe, split firewood.

I do not stuff sage in pig guts,
yet never flinch from mess. Just blood.
Dot watched my mother's smooth white gloves,
said nothing, marched to bus stops, strong
before heat soared. She chopped, heaved wood,
hacked pigs, lugged pails. She lived as long.

Cheesecakes

This recipe is a fake! Let me re-phrase that: a re-creation of cakes that have nothing to do with cheese. Many of Dot's early recipes are for cakes or puddings I never ate. But this is a recipe for small pastries which I *did* eat many times at Sunday tea-time. They were a favourite, though they had none of the 1950s evil glamour of icing sugar and butter cream, or even the richness of her dark 'Chocolate Mould' (blancmange).

The name 'Cheesecakes' may hark back to a farm recipe which used up spare milk curds. A Leicester bakery still makes a traditional pastry topped with curds. The cheesecakes made by Dot (and by my own mother) retained the pastry base and jam filling—but no curd cheese.

The topping on my mother's cheesecakes contained coconut, and was light and pleasant. But I secretly preferred Dot's. Her pastry was more filling, her plum jam was home-made and her topping was browner and nuttier. What was the extra ingredient? I think it may have been ground rice, a favourite staple in her Edwardian youth cooking for a 'family in Nottingham'. So I tried this, and liked it. But you could add desiccated coconut, or ground almond (the rich man's version of ground rice), or ground hazelnuts in place of the ground rice. Dot kept adapting recipes. So can we.

These little tarts are similar to what are more commonly known as 'Maids of Honour'. Just occasionally a Maids of Honour recipe will incorporate cheese curd.

INGREDIENTS

(makes 12-14 cheesecakes)

Pastry

3 oz / 60 g self-raising flour
3 oz / 60 g plain flour
3 oz / 60 g butter or lard
Pinch of salt
1-2 tablespoons cold water & squeeze of lemon juice to mix.

Topping

Good quality (preferably home-made) jam
1 egg, and the weight of the egg (roughly 2 oz or 30 g) for each of the following:

- golden caster sugar
- butter
- self-raising flour—but subtract ½ oz/10 g of this and replace with the same weight of ground rice.

EQUIPMENT

Wooden spoon (or hand-held mixer!)
Rolling pin
Mince pie tin.
Circular scone/biscuit cutter

METHOD

1. Pre-heat oven to 200°C/ 400°F / Gas Mark 6.
2. Make the pastry (using the method on page 23 for Bakewell Pudding).
3. Roll out the pastry to the thickness of roughly a £1.00 coin.
4. Cut pastry into circles with the scone cutter and line the tart bases in the mince pie tin, making sure it comes up the sides and creates a deep base.

CHEESECAKE METHOD (*cont.*)

5. Add about one generous teaspoon of jam and spread out a little.
6. Place the mince pie tin with cheesecake bases in refrigerator or cool place while you make the topping.
7. Weigh the topping ingredients.
8. Mix the flour and ground rice thoroughly.
9. Cream the margarine and sugar together with a wooden spoon until pale and fluffy.
10. Beat the egg well.
11. Add the egg gradually, beating the mixture well with each addition, and adding a teaspoonful of the ground rice/flour if it shows the least signs of curdling.
12. Sieve the ground rice / flour mixture over the top of the egg mixture and fold in carefully with a metal spoon.
13. Spoon this topping mixture over the jam in each cheesecake base—2-3 generous teaspoonfuls.
14. Spread gently with a knife to encourage the topping to reach the edge, but don't worry too much because it will quickly rise and spread in the oven.
15. Place in oven and bake for 15 minutes (could take a little longer, depending on your oven).
16. Topping should be well-risen, golden brown and firm to the touch.

PASSED

Her mother, ear pierced by a bee,
lay still before sun fell from sky.
Who was the mystery Aunt Polly
who had the studio portrait done
of Dot, crop-haired, with Miriam,
who, torn by her first son, would die?

Bustling, Dot spoke infrequently
of the lost farm, a dream, a breath
extinguished by Grandfather's death.
She kept the broad farm desk. It took
dog food and bills. It watched her cook.
In its dark drawers they found her book.

THE LINCOLNSHIRE CHRONICLE

You found a hobby: funerals.
The village taxi (Mr Hall's),
sailed to your door to take you there
while your son rode to the Game Fair
one holiday. You unpeeled notes
from your upright, moth-guarded coats.

Sometimes you crossed two towns by bus.
My doting father frowned at fuss.
They're all Dad's family. And why
doesn't she go when they're alive?
I think he missed the point. For sure
you met them at the wake before,

talked in front rooms, with creaking floors,
chewed pastries heavier than yours.
The women chose their corners. Men
just held by suits, tears dried by sun,
were spared from tractor seat or forge,
named, like my father, *Harold*, *George*,

the Cousins. So when you returned,
your bus ticket and black coat earned
one radiant hour at Sunday tea,
telling my father all you'd seen.
You know him, Harold!
The butcher?
No,
they say he flitted. Nelly's Joe—

You ticked them off on fingers, rapt,
as my bored father's best shoes tapped,
and you gazed at the *Chronicle*
which sang you each fresh funeral.
Children were sheltered. I—kept out—
did not see you flit from your house.

Fred lived for only two more years.
With funeral hands too full for tears,
I swayed in heels down backyard steps,
and offered ham, my mother's cakes,
to tall men, from crew-yard or forge,
called *Harold*, mostly (sometimes *George*).

Flamberries Pudding

Dot has defeated Google! No 'Flamberries'. Is it an old word for raspberries? Or for the swirling jam in this pudding (which my husband loved)?

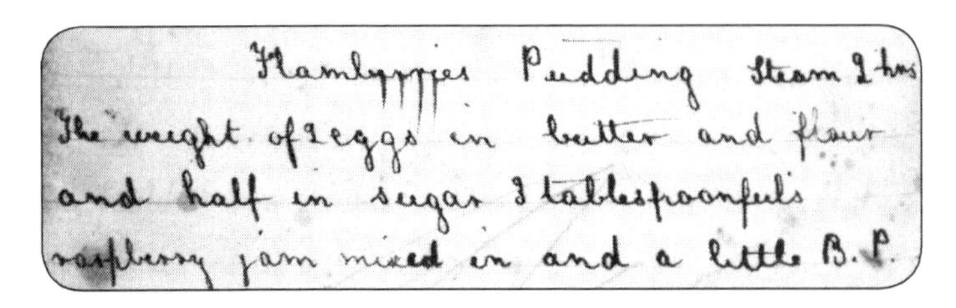

Flamberries Pudding Steam 2 hrs
The weight of 2 eggs in butter and flour
and half in sugar 3 tablespoonfuls
raspberry jam mixed in and a little B.P.

DOT'S ORIGINAL RECIPE

Flamberries Pudding Steam 2 hrs
The weight of 2 eggs in butter and flour
and half in sugar 3 tablespoonfuls
raspberry jam mixed in and a little B.P.

My version:

INGREDIENTS

1 egg (medium or large)
Its weight in softened butter
Its weight in self-raising flour
Half its weight in caster sugar
Generous 1½ tablespoonfuls of raspberry jam.

EQUIPMENT

Heat-proof basin 1 pt / 568 ml
Greaseproof paper, foil and string to cover the bowl.
Wooden spoon or hand-held mixer.
Large saucepan with lid, big enough to hold the basin easily when steaming

METHOD

1. Weigh softened butter, put in mixing bowl and cut into small pieces.
2. Prepare paper, foil and string ready to cover the basin and tie neatly in place (if you haven't done this before, check out videos online which will show you step by step).
3. Cream butter, with spoon or hand-held mixer, until pale and fluffy.
4. Weigh sugar and beat it into butter.
5. Weigh and sift flour.
6. Beat egg. Add egg and a little flour to the butter and sugar mixture, stirring with wooden spoon. Then add rest of flour and fold in lightly with metal spoon.
7. Stir in jam lightly, just enough to leave the pudding veined with it.
8. Spoon mixture into basin. Smooth top of mixture.
9. Put greaseproof paper and foil over the top and tie with string.
10. Place in large saucepan with enough simmering water to come half way up the basin. Put lid on tightly.
11. Simmer on low heat for 1½ hours. (Or, if you have a steamer, cook on top layer following steamer instructions for same length of time.)
12. Serve with custard (or cream).

WARNING!

I burnt my mouth with this pudding. The veins of jam are MUCH hotter than the sponge pudding. Leave each helping to cool for a few minutes in its bowl. Eat with caution. Looks messy. Tastes delicious!

OUT

Dot booked trips, to her men's surprise.
Her hat, the careful blue of eyes,
was skewered by pearl pins to her bun.
The '20s roared past her, were gone.

It was the Mothers' Union bus
which bore her off to potteries
through Spalding tulips in the spring,
Holland's black stamens glistening.

She brought us presents: blue-glazed jars,
small trophies from her final wars.
At four, in starched dark, her heart stopped.
Her tall son groped to the phone box.

I studied, then, did not learn how
verse comes from *versus*, turn of plough.
My father, ploughboy once, wrote verse.
I did not see dark gloves or hearse,

stepped back too late through her low door,
glimpsed rose and blue, in new dusts, saw
before her last bus lurched homewards
she'd bought herself two china birds.

BEFORE DAWN

Nottingham. Basement. Chimes. How could
you slicetoastfryboilcoaxdampwood
then   breakfastcleared   teagulped   begin
potatoespeeled   greetbutcher'sboy
twistpastryleavesonlunchtimepie
whipsponge   spreadteascones? My head spins.

My teacher-mother met your son,
watched you, in winter, move house: one
husband, three grown children; thinner,
scrub black from beams, chop crusts for dogs,
whisk cloth-capped pudding from your box,
steambasteserve hugeChristmasdinner.

How quickly time beat through your day;
how slowly for your youngest boy.
The high clock's hour-hand heaved, then dropped
across your wall. Your men, at four,
trooped down the hills to winter's door.
Youwashedpotswoundclocks   slept   You stopped.

ON HORKSTOW HILL

House-moving was called flitting and
your flitting crossed half Lincolnshire
until your shepherd husband saw
the best show flock, on Horkstow Hill.

Well, Fred is married to the sheep.
You had your men and house to keep
but could be sometimes lonely, while the deep
horse chestnut shadows swept the sill.

I came to visit for a day.
Red conker flowers blew past your gate
where Toots, the old dog, waited, chained
by the back door, too stiff for hills.

The morning washed us like a dream.
I must have read. You chopped, boiled, cleaned,
scoured pans, quick cook. Small windows flared,
late summer sun soared on the hill.

We'll have a walk, you told me then.
Go up the hill and find the men.
You clamped your hat on like the Queen.
Your village slept, one street. Yet still

women came out, to nod to you,
to ask about my life. I knew
I was your prize show lamb. But soon
we caught the wind and climbed the hill.

Although I wanted most to keep
close by the men, the half-clipped sheep,
I saw broad Humber shine beneath,
and small heartsease, at corn's edge, spill.

I never realised you were old.
You marched back, cooked huge tea. In folds
muddied as love, the Humber rolled
as we climbed Horkstow Hill.

Vinegar Cake

This is a war-time recipe. Vinegar and baking soda combine to create lightness (instead of eggs that would have been hard to come by). Dot would have used malt vinegar but any will do the chemical trick required (I used sherry vinegar). The cake is very good and doesn't taste in the least vinegary! My version reduces the sugar, increases the fruit and cooks at lower heat. Best eaten fresh but will keep for a few days. Nice with butter.

DOT'S ORIGINAL RECIPE

Mix 1 lb of flour, 1 teaspoon B.P. one of
bar-soda together well rub in ¼ lb butter
or dripping. add ½ lb sultanas 6 oz
brown sugar, well mix with ½ pint
lukewarm milk add 1 tablespoonful
vinegar after beating well
Bake 2 hours in moderate oven.

My version:

INGREDIENTS

8 oz / 225 g self-raising flour
¾ teaspoon bicarbonate of soda
2 oz / 55 g softened butter (or marg or lard)
8 oz / 225 g mixed dried fruit (figs/dates add richness)
1½ oz / 40 g caster sugar
¼ pint / ⅛ litre lukewarm milk
¾ tablespoon vinegar

EQUIPMENT

7" deep baking tin
Wooden spoon or large fork to mix

METHOD

1. Pre-heat oven to 160°C / 325°F / Gas Mark 3.
2. Grease baking tin and then dust with flour to create a non-stick surface.
3. Weigh flour and add fat cut in small pieces. Rub fat into flour with finger tips.
4. Weigh dried fruit and sugar and mix in.
5. Warm milk to blood heat, add bicarbonate of soda, beat with a fork and add to the flour/fruit mixture, beating all well together.
6. Once the cake mixture is well mixed, beat in the vinegar.
7. Bake for approximately one hour..
8. Test after an hour with a skewer. It will come out clean if cake is done.
9. Allow to cool slightly in the tin, then turn out onto a wire rack.
10. The top looks very plain, but one option is to ice while warm with a little water icing made with three tablespoons or so of icing sugar and lemon juice to mix.
11. Eat when cold.

SUNDAY NIGHT

Never go back. Once on a screen
I found Horkstow. Horse chestnut trees,
saplings their farmer set, loomed high.

New houses flew at me till, shocked,
I reared back like a horse, so stopped
before their house flashed, just in time.

Because, I think, they still lean there
replete with tea, the range's glow
sunk soft. The two who raise great sheep

grumble at lack of swedes. The son
whose mind sleeps, nods, idly benign.
Dot sits, sharp as the collies. She

flew downstairs when, at ten to four,
a lorry brought a son from war,
my father, shrapnel in his neck.

Now, unrouged face as fresh as rain
she springs when we rise, finds a tin,
the best nut toffee safely kept.

Horkstow lies dark as wartime still.
Below the flock and limestone hill
her wild white bluebells wake night air.

The chestnut, which makes low roofs black,
bends to me. I need not go back.
Because I hope you are still there.
Because I know you are still there.

YOUR GREAT-GRANDDAUGHTER COOKS

If offered peppered rocket leaf;
green olive oil you used to keep
for ears; light buns with blueberries;
smooth pasta; soft Italian cheese;
German red cabbage, simmered hours;
sage leaf fried crisp—
                                        if, lit by flowers,
your plate was set, what would you do?

Taste each fresh mouthful, wonderingly.
Then ask her for the recipe.

NOTE ON DOT'S LIFE

DOROTHY ELIZA BARNES, my father's mother, was born on November 28th, 1894. I learned this from the dashing, blotched writing of her own grandmother, Eliza Reed, at the front of the family Bible. How could the first Eliza afford this great embossed edition, which I can scarcely lift? It came from the Lost Farm. Many farmworkers' families, in my childhood, carried with them the story of the Lost Farm. Some may have been myths. But I once saw a photograph of Eliza's: a brick house, set on the bare farmland of Lincolnshire, with one wind-bent tree. Eliza's Bible records, in a steady hand, that her husband, Joseph, died at forty-three. I suspect the farm went with him.

So the farm gave Eliza the Bible. But why did Eliza give the Bible, 'With Love', to her small namesake—my grandmother and the daughter of Eliza's youngest daughter, Louisa—on her first birthday in Sutton-on-Sea in 1895? Louisa had married a farm labourer: John Maiden Barnes. (I still have his ditching tools, stamped with his initials.) Dot was her second daughter. Somehow, even then, baby Dot had become the one who would carry the weight of the family forward. She was to be the only long-term survivor. Miriam, her elder sister, died in childbirth in the 1930s. Dot recorded her sister's death at the foot of the Bible's first page, in tiny writing.

Louisa, Dot's mother, did not live to be old. When only a young mother, she was stung in the ear by a bee and was dead, my father said, by nightfall. Miriam and Dot (not yet three) appear in a photograph, two small shocked girls with brushed cropped hair, standing by a smart woman in black. This was 'Aunt Polly', a mysterious figure who could afford studio portraits of a farm labourer's daughters. Was Aunt Polly the old lady who used to clean her range flues by stuffing them with gunpowder, then lighting a paper fuse? Dot, sent to the village shop to buy the gunpowder, was still radiant sixty years later when she described the excitement of that sootfall.

Dot acquired a stepmother and new siblings, including her step-sisters, Fanny and Nellie. They were prettier and dressier than Dot.

My two great-aunts showed great kindness to my family; less to each other. After their father's death, the Great Row About The Sewing Machine kept Nellie and Fanny apart for three decades. Yet, separately, they always came from their Midland towns to Dot's warm room and cake-laden table.

Dot never spoke to me about her working life before marriage. My father would say proudly: *Mother was Cook for a family in Nottingham.* The census which might list Dorothy Eliza Barnes, Cook, is still locked away. I don't know whether she worked in a tall terraced tradesman's house, or in one of the grander red-brick villas which still stand at the edge of Nottingham. I do know that the family was lucky to have Dot, her exceptional steadiness, cleverness—and puddings.

Once, as we were leaving at the end of a Sunday visit, Dot suddenly said to me, *What people say about the summer before the First World War is true. It was the most beautiful summer I have ever seen.* Why did she say that, rummaging in the tin for my favourite nut toffee on a stormy Lincolnshire night? Had she lost the man she loved? Or simply years of her life, cooking ingeniously with dried egg in a basement in Nottingham?

Five years after the war, she married my grandfather. She was twenty-eight. My other grandmother, whose wedding came before the war, was much younger when she married. I realise, poring over Dot's carefully inked dates, that she and I both lived for almost three decades before bearing our first child.

Dot's husband, Fred Brackenbury, was a couple of years younger. He was as tall as Dot was tiny, and came from a long line of prize-winning shepherds. Fred told me, with quiet pride, *My father was a shepherd, and my grandfather—and mebbe my great-grandfather....*

He was, my grandmother complained, married to the sheep. My father remembered bitterly that if his father decided his show flock wasn't getting enough food, he would find another job and that meant they would have to move to yet another cottage with soot-blackened beams for my grandmother to sluice clean.

My father's schooldays were spent in more Lincolnshire villages than I can name: Bigby, Brocklesby, Riby.... Sometimes they lived on outlying 'granges', miles from the village, so my grandmother would push her youngest son to school in a pram. But Dot, small as a wren, and with the same fierce energy, may have shared her husband's restlessness. *When we lived at Riby,* my father said despairingly, *we even moved across the YARD!*

Dot and Fred had four children. Their father, a member of that strange village aristocracy of skilled, upright workers, could be curt and domineering—yet they called him 'Dad'. But Dot was always referred to, with a reverent slowing of breath, as 'Mother'. I knew my aunt and uncles as shy adults. I also saw photographs of them, as surprisingly lively children, on windswept fields like Eliza's farm, or by the great dykes in which one of them nearly drowned—his brother, just in time, saw the bobble of his hat, knitted by Dot, floating past.

Nora, the eldest, never married, and, as far as I know, never worked. Perhaps Dot, the motherless child sent out to 'service', did not want her daughter to do the same. Perhaps she liked to have Nora with her in the kitchens of those isolated cottages, and came to think of her as a replacement housekeeper for her father and brothers.

So Nora, awkwardly tall, with fine hair and crooked teeth, stayed by Dot's side until it became clear that she was terribly ill. She raged and swore at her mother. The doctors decided she had an incurable brain tumour. Nora went away to various institutions, visited by her family, until she died, aged thirty-eight. My grandfather said that he had cried all his tears for her already, every morning, on the paths up the hill to the sheep. When we went to Sunday tea for the first time after Nora's death, Dot was quiet, but she brightened when my sister and I rushed into her dark kitchen. She was still enveloped in a clean, pressed, flowered pinafore, as though in her cook's uniform. Her table was full of cake.

Dot's youngest child was Owen. (Mysteriously, each of her sons' names came from a different British kingdom. My father was Harold, an English name which crowded his father's family. Her second son was called Gordon.)

Owen's birth, when she was forty-one, seems to have caused serious damage. Dauntless as she was, Dot had to stay in bed for weeks with the baby. The most perfect mothers can be the most destructive. She stayed too close to Owen. Academically the brightest, the child who smiled most broadly in those remote fields, he failed his exams at sixteen, could not work with his father, did National Service and grew depressed in a job as an Army clerk in dark stores. The electric shock treatments of the 1950s left him an amiable, if sometimes anxious shadow. He lived at home, with strong medication, and hand-knitted pullovers. Dot and Fred refused ever to draw a penny of State benefits for him.

These are the dark pages of Dot's family Bible. Like her grandmother, in Bibles or recipe books, she would draw a firm line beneath an entry. I do not remember my grandmother and her family as unhappy. I remember all of them, Fred with his pipe in his high-backed chair, Dot on her stool, Owen under the clock, Gordon at the table with his elbow by the teapot, telling stories in their slow, soft-edged Lincolnshire voices, poking the small furnace of their fire, and laughing.

Gordon was a handsome man, loved especially by children. He was his father's heir. For a quarter of a century after Fred's death, Gordon continued to win almost every prize at the Royal Show for his employer's flock of Romney Marsh sheep, beating off the Kent shepherds.

For the last twenty years of my grandmother's life the family finally settled, in a tiny village called Horkstow, under the shadow of a limestone ridge where the sheep lived.

Gordon never married, but he always had friends, both men and women. A married female friend, a dog trainer, drove him, as an old man, to a Sheep Society dinner where, to the diners' amazement, he made a fluent and witty speech entirely from memory. In his own world, like his father before him, he was a king. There are worse lives.

My father, who hated sheep, had left home at fourteen to become a ploughboy. He survived the kicks of Shire horses—and one capsized cart—until the Second World War. His neck was hit by shrapnel as the infantry ran, wild boar fleeing before them, through the forests of the Ardennes. When an army lorry dropped him off on leave, in the middle of an unlit, strange English village in the early hours of the morning, Dot flew downstairs and flung open the door of their latest, tiny farm cottage. Without letter, telephone or email, she'd known he was home.

Betty Powell, the schoolgirl who was to be my mother, lived in that village. She and my father met at a party in a house on the limestone ridge, the Cliff. My mother (who shared my talent for confusion) thought that my father, who inherited Dot's handsome waves of hair, was the cousin of a village boy, a glamorous guest from Grimsby. Betty (a gamekeeper's daughter) went off to train as a teacher in London but after a long engagement she married my father. He had learnt to drive in the army and became a farm lorry driver for forty years, working for the same wealthy landowner as his own father. My parents stayed in the village where they had met until they retired. My father then dug a new vegetable garden and learnt to play golf. A BBC radio presenter met him on the course, and described him on air as *a seventy-five year old skipping around like a spring lamb.*

How did Dot feed her children so well? Fred, after long hours with the sheep, went out after tea to work in the vegetable garden. Dot was a marvel with money. My father said she would pack coal dust into blue paper sugar bags to burn on the fire. On a shepherd's wage, with two dependent adult children, she squirrelled away savings in the Post Office, which grew into tens of thousands of pounds. She could have bought her own house in Horkstow. A stone cottage by a dyke came up for sale. It cost, I think, two thousand pounds. Dot had two thousand pounds. She kept walking down to look at the place, but did not buy it. Perhaps she guessed, correctly, that Gordon, preoccupied by his sheep, would never maintain a house. Her only failure of organisation was not to make a will, which cost my father hours of driving *his* father and brothers to country solicitors.

Dot's later life, without her daughter, could be lonely, my father thought. When the children of a Polish farm worker waited for the school bus by her gate, she would call them in and give them sweets. Horkstow shrank. The local paper ran an article, marvelling at its one street, and its tiny Mothers' Union. My grandmother became the surprise star of this article, with her frank remarks about her traditional farm-working family: 'the men'. *Fred is married to the sheep. And Gordon is even worse. It's lucky he's a bachelor....* My sister found this article. I don't recall 'the men's reaction. I expect they eyed their home-made pastries, huge fruit cake, Dot's delicious dark blancmange with tinned pears, and decided not to make too much fuss.

I remember that blancmange, called prosaically 'Chocolate Mould'. In Dot's Nottingham days, I would guess she had to turn it out—perilously—from a fluted copper mould. It was rich with cocoa, far less sweet than many of the treats of the sugar-crazed 1950s. I remember her cooking, simply, as perfect. She told me, proudly, that she always mixed plain and self-raising flour for her airy pastry. (I was shocked when I first chewed through the leathery mince pies donated to our village Christmas parties.) Almost everything was homemade. Somehow, in treeless Lincolnshire, she found Victoria plums every year, and filled shelves with the amber of plum jam. It was the only jam my grandfather liked. They had grown together in habits, like two trees at a farm gate.

My sister and daughter, like my mother, are excellent cooks. I inherited the desk (from the Lost Farm?), which had travelled with Dot in farm carts and lorries on all her moves. Inside it, I keep the battered black notebook my parents found, full of Dot's recipes. She must have begun this book when she started her job in Nottingham as a young cook. Dot's lovely blue eyes were short-sighted. In the smallest script, she has faithfully copied her family's favourites: *Aunt Margaret's Pudding....*

Puddings, indeed have priority. There are thirteen of them at the start of Dot's notebook. Her Christmas pudding recipe would fill six basins. There are thirty-three cakes: *Buttermilk Cake, Treacle Scones, Chocolate Cake, Coffee Cake....* That fortunate Nottingham family could never have been bored at tea time. There are also ingredients for embrocation, for a tired cook's back: ½ pt raw linseed oil, 1 oz oil of thyme.

For some staples, like mincemeat, Dot has collected many recipes, in various hands. There is a boldly written recipe for wine, which I think came from a neighbour, during her afterlife as a shepherd's wife. The large round letters of 'Biscuits' may be Nora's. The book, smudged from steamy kitchens, once scribbled on by a child, is a glimpse of the busy shared lives of women. This lost country generation's lives were quiet, but rich with old knowledge and individual talent. They were writers, too, and they recorded their skills. Dot kept both her weighty dark Bible and her own black notebook of recipes.

I am not nostalgic for their lives. I have seen tiny photographs from the 1920s, in which both Dot and her husband Fred look half-starved. Her mother might have been saved by anti-histamines, her sister by a caesarean section. But I think more and more of the virtues of Dot's generation. This admiration may have helped thwart some of my parents' ambitions for me.

Dot, as a married woman, always lived in small houses. The Lost Farm, and later difficulties in her own family, left her wary of social climbing. She preferred to live with unpretentious, hard-working people. When she went out—which she loved—she usually walked or travelled on buses. She was frugal with money, and never threw out food (the sheep dogs got the crusts).

Yet she was notably generous with gifts. She and her neighbours saved each other. While Dot lay sick in bed after the birth of her fourth child, a neighbour cooked and washed—for weeks—for Dot's husband and three children. Dot herself fed the jobless men who tramped round Lincolnshire farms in the 1930s. I have known women in my suburb who scarcely speak to the family next door. Dot was greatly admired by her neighbours. I will never be her equal in practical generosity.

Yet, back from the bus, in my small house, I write at her desk and think of her often, with gratitude.

After all her years of cooking, scrubbing, hacking up pig carcasses and baking fruit cakes all night for 'the men' to take to the Royal Show, Dot lived to be seventy-six. One January night she died, as she had lived, quietly, and without fuss.

Her pantry shelves were full.